THIS BOOK BELONGS TO

_____

START DATE

_____

EDITORIAL

EDITORS-IN-CHIEF
Raechel Myers & Amanda Bible Williams

CONTENT DIRECTOR
Russ Ramsey, MDiv., ThM.

MANAGING EDITOR
Jessica Lamb

EDITORS
Kara Gause
Melanie Rainer

EDITORIAL ASSISTANT
Ellen Taylor

CREATIVE

CREATIVE DIRECTOR
Ryan Myers

ART DIRECTOR & DESIGNER
Kelsea Allen

ILLUSTRATOR
Emily Knapp

COVER PHOTOGRAPHER
Michaela Harbison

PHOTOGRAPHERS
Abigail Bobo (4, 69)
Michaela Harbison (17, 21, 27, 47, 51, 65)
Nicola Harger (31)
Liz Rudman (55)

All photography used by permission.

◉ ▼ ⨍

@SHEREADSTRUTH

SHEREADSTRUTH.COM

SUBSCRIPTION INQUIRIES
orders@shereadstruth.com

SHE READS TRUTH™

© 2018 by She Reads Truth, LLC

All rights reserved.

ISBN 978-1-946282-78-1

No part of this publication may be reproduced, distributed, or transmitted in any form or by any means, including photocopying, recording, or other electronic or mechanical methods, without the prior written permission of She Reads Truth, LLC, except in the case of brief quotations embodied in critical reviews and certain other noncommercial uses permitted by copyright law.

All Scripture is taken from the Christian Standard Bible®. Copyright © 2017 by Holman Bible Publishers. Used by permission. Christian Standard Bible® and CSB® are federally registered trademarks of Holman Bible Publishers.

This book was printed offset in Nashville, Tennessee, on 70# Lynx Opaque. Cover is 100# Cougar Opaque with a soft touch lamination.

THIS IS
THE GOSPEL

EDITOR'S LETTER

> **The gospel is the great leveler.**

I grew up going to church and learning the story of Jesus. I have always known it. I cannot remember a time when God or the Bible was new to me. Yet somehow in my thirty-five years, time after time, the reality of my brokenness and Christ's work on my behalf takes my breath away. It feels brand new.

I have a number of people in my life who are not believers. Women at my gym, in my neighborhood, and in broader friend circles. When I think about the question, "What is the gospel?", I think about how I can share it with them. Of course the gospel is complex—even mysterious. Explaining it can be intimidating. But the gospel is also beautifully simple. As someone who has confessed with my mouth and believes in my heart that Jesus saved me, I should be able to share what I believe with anyone who asks. Even if they're asking mid-Pilates-workout.

This book is for people who don't believe. It is for seekers and shruggers and strugglers. It's for the girl who thinks God might be too complicated, or too simple. It's for the woman who is intimidated by the Bible, but wants to know what it says. And it's for the one who has heard the word "gospel" all her life, but if she's honest, can't quite tell you what it means.

This book is also for believers. Christians need to remember the truth of the gospel every single day. We need to preach it to ourselves and to each other, rehearsing the story of why we need saving and how Jesus saved us. We need to understand the significance of the cross so we can remember where our hope lies.

This book is for you. Whatever your story, wherever you've been, you are neither disqualified nor overqualified. The gospel is the great leveler. Jesus invites everyone to repent and believe the good news.

My prayer as you read this book is that you would come to understand the gospel in a deeper way. That when someone asks you, or you need to remind yourself, you can point to God's Word in this book and answer, "This is the gospel."

Grace & Peace,

Raechel Myers
EDITOR-IN-CHIEF

DESIGN ON PURPOSE

"

The branch for redemption is our favorite, which uses a bandage to represent the grafting of our old lives to new life in Christ.

The gospel is for everyone. We designed this book to represent that truth, to feel universally approachable and inviting. The photography depicts kitchens, porches, and backyards—the settings of our lives and the places where we live out our faith every day.

In order to highlight Scripture with minimal distractions, we limited our color palette to only black and beige. We simplified our design by using just two fonts: Garamond and Futura. Garamond is the font we use for daily Scripture reading in every study book, but this time, we used it for day titles as well. These day titles are worded to tell the story of the gospel when read in sequence.

This two-week reading plan is divided into four sections, represented symbolically by the branch illustrations you'll first see on the "This Is the Gospel" extra on pages 12–15. Our in-house artist created these branch illustrations to show the progression of our journey with Christ, a journey that is both a shared experience for believers throughout history and unique in each of our lives. The branch for redemption is our favorite, which uses a bandage to represent the grafting of our old lives to new life in Christ.

Simple, airy spreads with callouts summarize each section, further emphasizing this progression and, in turn, the gospel narrative. As you read, we hope these choices serve as a reminder of both the simple wonder and deep power of the gospel.

THE SHE READS TRUTH CREATIVE TEAM

HOW TO USE THIS BOOK

She Reads Truth is a community of women dedicated to reading the Word of God every day.

The Bible is living and active, breathed out by God, and we confidently hold it higher than anything we can do or say. This book focuses primarily on Scripture, with bonus resources to facilitate deeper engagement with God's Word.

SCRIPTURE READING

Designed for a Monday start, this study book presents the gospel of Jesus Christ in daily Scripture readings.

JOURNALING SPACE

Each weekday features space for personal reflection and prayer.

GRACE DAY

Use Saturdays to pray, rest, and reflect on what you've read.

For added community and conversation, join us in the **This Is the Gospel** reading plan on the She Reads Truth app or at SheReadsTruth.com.

WEEKLY TRUTH

Sundays are set aside for weekly Scripture memorization.

Find the corresponding memory cards in the back of this book.

SHE READS TRUTH

TABLE OF CONTENTS

Week 1

CREATION

16	**DAY 1**	*God Created the Heavens and the Earth*
20	**DAY 2**	*God Created Mankind in His Image*

FALL

26	**DAY 3**	*Humanity Rebelled Against God*
30	**DAY 4**	*All People Are Sinful by Nature*
36	**DAY 5**	*We Cannot Save Ourselves*
40	**DAY 6**	*Grace Day*
42	**DAY 7**	*Weekly Truth*

EXTRAS   10   *This Is the Gospel*   34   *The Person of Jesus*

Week 2

REDEMPTION

46	DAY 8	*Jesus Lived, Died, and Rose from the Grave*
50	DAY 9	*Jesus Calls Us to Faith and Repentance*
54	DAY 10	*We Are Saved by Grace Through Faith*

RESTORATION

64	DAY 11	*Jesus Secures Our Peace with God*
68	DAY 12	*All Creation Will Be Restored*
72	DAY 13	*Grace Day*
74	DAY 14	*Weekly Truth*

58	*The Work of Jesus*	76	*Invitation*	80	*For the Record*

THIS IS THE GOSPEL

The gospel is the good news of what Jesus Christ has done to restore broken creation and sinful people to their holy Creator. It is the true story of humankind's relationship with God, which is marred by sin and restored by grace through faith in Christ alone. The following Scripture verses summarize the gospel in four parts: creation, fall, redemption, and restoration.

CREATION

God is the infinite, eternal Creator of all things.
HEB 11:3

God created the heavens and the earth, and He made them good.
GN 1:1–31

God created humanity in His own image and likeness.
GN 1:27

We were created to love, obey, worship, and be in a relationship with God, our Maker.
MC 6:8

FALL

Adam and Eve, our first parents, turned away from God and rebelled against Him.
GN 3:1–7

When humanity rebelled against God, all creation became subject to death, decay, and frustration.
RM 8:20

We all have inherited this sinful nature, and we are unable to obey God perfectly.
IS 53:6

The penalty for sin is death, and we are unable to save ourselves.
RM 6:23

REDEMPTION

God responded to our need for salvation by sending His only Son, Jesus Christ, to live as one of us.
1JN 4:14

Jesus came to deliver us from our sin and restore order and peace to the world.
COL 1:19–20

Jesus lived, died, and rose from the dead as the perfect substitute for us.
1PT 2:24

We are saved by grace through faith in Jesus.
EPH 2:6–9

RESTORATION

Jesus restores us to God by securing our relationship with God forever. We receive Christ's righteousness and are presented as holy and blameless before God.
COL 1:21–23

Christians play a role in God's restoring work in the world through loving and serving both God and neighbor.
MT 5:16

Jesus reigns as King over all creation, with all authority and power forever.
COL 1:15–18

One day all creation will be perfectly restored, and Jesus will make everything new.
RV 21:1–5

CREATION

God saw all that he had made,
and it was very good indeed.

GENESIS 1:31

DAY 1

GOD CREATED THE HEAVENS AND THE EARTH

Genesis 1:1–25; Isaiah 45:12; John 1:1–5; Hebrews 11:3

GENESIS 1:1–25
The Creation

¹ In the beginning God created the heavens and the earth.

² Now the earth was formless and empty, darkness covered the surface of the watery depths, and the Spirit of God was hovering over the surface of the waters. ³ Then God said, "Let there be light," and there was light. ⁴ God saw that the light was good, and God separated the light from the darkness. ⁵ God called the light "day," and the darkness he called "night." There was an evening, and there was a morning: one day.

⁶ Then God said, "Let there be an expanse between the waters, separating water from water." ⁷ So God made the expanse and separated the water under the expanse from the water above the expanse. And it was so. ⁸ God called the expanse "sky." Evening came and then morning: the second day.

⁹ Then God said, "Let the water under the sky be gathered into one place, and let the dry land appear." And it was so. ¹⁰ God called the dry land "earth," and the gathering of the water he called "seas." And God saw that it was good. ¹¹ Then God said, "Let the earth produce vegetation: seed-bearing plants and fruit trees on the earth bearing fruit with seed in it according to their kinds." And it was so. ¹² The earth produced vegetation: seed-bearing plants according to their kinds and trees bearing fruit with seed in it according to their kinds. And God saw that it was good. ¹³ Evening came and then morning: the third day.

¹⁴ Then God said, "Let there be lights in the expanse of the sky to separate the day from the night. They will serve as signs for seasons and for days and years. ¹⁵ They will be lights in the expanse of the sky to provide light on the earth." And it was so. ¹⁶ God made the two great lights—the greater light to rule over the day and the lesser light to rule over the night—as well as the stars. ¹⁷ God placed them in the expanse of the sky to provide light on the earth, ¹⁸ to rule the day and the night, and to separate light from darkness. And God saw that it was good. ¹⁹ Evening came and then morning: the fourth day.

²⁰ Then God said, "Let the water swarm with living creatures, and let birds fly above the earth across the expanse of the sky." ²¹ So God created the large sea-creatures and every living creature that moves and swarms in the water, according to their kinds. He also created every winged creature according to its kind. And God saw that it was good. ²² God blessed them: "Be fruitful, multiply, and fill the waters of the seas, and let the birds multiply on the earth." ²³ Evening came and then morning: the fifth day.

²⁴ Then God said, "Let the earth produce living creatures according to their kinds: livestock, creatures that crawl, and the wildlife of the earth according to their kinds." And it was so. ²⁵ So God made the wildlife of the earth according to their kinds, the livestock according to their kinds, and all the creatures that crawl on the ground according to their kinds. And God saw that it was good.

ISAIAH 45:12
"I made the earth,
and created humans on it.
It was my hands that stretched out the heavens,
and I commanded everything in them."

JOHN 1:1–5
Prologue

¹ In the beginning was the Word, and the Word was with God, and the Word was God. ² He was with God in the beginning. ³ All things were created through him, and apart from him not one thing was created that has been created. ⁴ In him was life, and that life was the light of men. ⁵ That light shines in the darkness, and yet the darkness did not overcome it.

HEBREWS 11:3
By faith we understand that the universe was created by the word of God, so that what is seen was made from things that are not visible.

NOTES

And God saw that it was good. GENESIS 1:10

DAY 2

GOD CREATED MANKIND IN HIS IMAGE

Genesis 1:26–31; Psalm 8; 1 Corinthians 15:47–49

GENESIS 1:26–31

²⁶ Then God said, "Let us make man in our image, according to our likeness. They will rule the fish of the sea, the birds of the sky, the livestock, the whole earth, and the creatures that crawl on the earth."

²⁷ So God created man in his own image;
he created him in the image of God;
he created them male and female.

²⁸ God blessed them, and God said to them, "Be fruitful, multiply, fill the earth, and subdue it. Rule the fish of the sea, the birds of the sky, and every creature that crawls on the earth." ²⁹ God also said, "Look, I have given you every seed-bearing plant on the surface of the entire earth and every tree whose fruit contains seed. This will be food for you, ³⁰ for all the wildlife of the earth, for every bird of the sky, and for every creature that crawls on the earth—everything having the breath of life in it—I have given every green plant for food." And it was so. ³¹ God saw all that he had made, and it was very good indeed. Evening came and then morning: the sixth day.

PSALM 8

God's Glory, Human Dignity
For the choir director: on the Gittith. A psalm of David.

¹ Lord, our Lord,
how magnificent is your name throughout the earth!
You have covered the heavens with your majesty.
² From the mouths of infants and nursing babies,
you have established a stronghold
on account of your adversaries
in order to silence the enemy and the avenger.

³ When I observe your heavens,
the work of your fingers,
the moon and the stars,
which you set in place,
⁴ what is a human being that you remember him,
a son of man that you look after him?
⁵ You made him little less than God
and crowned him with glory and honor.
⁶ You made him ruler over the works of your hands;
you put everything under his feet:
⁷ all the sheep and oxen,
as well as the animals in the wild,
⁸ the birds of the sky,
and the fish of the sea
that pass through the currents of the seas.

⁹ Lord, our Lord,
how magnificent is your name throughout the earth!

1 CORINTHIANS 15:47–49

⁴⁷ The first man was from the earth, a man of dust; the second man is from heaven. ⁴⁸ Like the man of dust, so are those who are of the dust; like the man of heaven, so are those who are of heaven. ⁴⁹ And just as we have borne the image of the man of dust, we will also bear the image of the man of heaven.

NOTES

What is a human being that you remember him, a son of man that you look after him? PSALM 8:4

FALL

They have abandoned the Lord;
they have despised the Holy One of Israel;
they have turned their backs on him.

ISAIAH 1:4

DAY 3

HUMANITY REBELLED AGAINST GOD

Genesis 3:1–19; Deuteronomy 28:15–19; Isaiah 1:4–5; Romans 5:12–14

GENESIS 3:1–19

The Temptation and the Fall

¹ Now the serpent was the most cunning of all the wild animals that the Lord God had made. He said to the woman, "Did God really say, 'You can't eat from any tree in the garden'?"

² The woman said to the serpent, "We may eat the fruit from the trees in the garden. ³ But about the fruit of the tree in the middle of the garden, God said, 'You must not eat it or touch it, or you will die.'"

⁴ "No! You will not die," the serpent said to the woman. ⁵ "In fact, God knows that when you eat it your eyes will be opened and you will be like God, knowing good and evil." ⁶ The woman saw that the tree was good for food and delightful to look at, and that it was desirable for obtaining wisdom. So she took some of its fruit and ate it; she also gave some to her husband, who was with her, and he ate it. ⁷ Then the eyes of both of them were opened, and they knew they were naked; so they sewed fig leaves together and made coverings for themselves.

Sin's Consequences

⁸ Then the man and his wife heard the sound of the Lord God walking in the garden at the time of the evening breeze, and they hid from the Lord God among the trees of the garden. ⁹ So the Lord God called out to the man and said to him, "Where are you?"

¹⁰ And he said, "I heard you in the garden, and I was afraid because I was naked, so I hid."

Continued

¹¹ Then he asked, "Who told you that you were naked? Did you eat from the tree that I commanded you not to eat from?"

¹² The man replied, "The woman you gave to be with me—she gave me some fruit from the tree, and I ate."

¹³ So the Lord God asked the woman, "What is this you have done?"

And the woman said, "The serpent deceived me, and I ate."

¹⁴ So the Lord God said to the serpent:

> Because you have done this,
> you are cursed more than any livestock
> and more than any wild animal.
> You will move on your belly
> and eat dust all the days of your life.
> ¹⁵ I will put hostility between you and the woman,
> and between your offspring and her offspring.
> He will strike your head,
> and you will strike his heel.

¹⁶ He said to the woman:

> I will intensify your labor pains;
> you will bear children with painful effort.
> Your desire will be for your husband,
> yet he will rule over you.

¹⁷ And he said to the man, "Because you listened to your wife and ate from the tree about which I commanded you, 'Do not eat from it':

> The ground is cursed because of you.
> You will eat from it by means of painful labor
> all the days of your life.
> ¹⁸ It will produce thorns and thistles for you,
> and you will eat the plants of the field.
> ¹⁹ You will eat bread by the sweat of your brow
> until you return to the ground,
> since you were taken from it.
> For you are dust,
> and you will return to dust."

DEUTERONOMY 28:15–19

¹⁵ "But if you do not obey the Lord your God by carefully following all his commands and statutes I am giving you today, all these curses will come and overtake you:

> ¹⁶ You will be cursed in the city
> and cursed in the country.
> ¹⁷ Your basket and kneading bowl will be cursed.
> ¹⁸ Your offspring will be cursed,
> and your land's produce,
> the young of your herds,
> and the newborn of your flocks.
> ¹⁹ You will be cursed when you come in
> and cursed when you go out."

ISAIAH 1:4–5

⁴ Oh sinful nation,
people weighed down with iniquity,
brood of evildoers,
depraved children!
They have abandoned the Lord;
they have despised the Holy One of Israel;
they have turned their backs on him.

⁵ Why do you want more beatings?
Why do you keep on rebelling?
The whole head is hurt,
and the whole heart is sick.

ROMANS 5:12–14

Death Through Adam and Life Through Christ

¹² Therefore, just as sin entered the world through one man, and death through sin, in this way death spread to all people, because all sinned. ¹³ In fact, sin was in the world before the law, but sin is not charged to a person's account when there is no law. ¹⁴ Nevertheless, death reigned from Adam to Moses, even over those who did not sin in the likeness of Adam's transgression. He is a type of the Coming One.

NOTES

―――

"What is this you have done?" GENESIS 3:13

DAY 4

ALL PEOPLE ARE SINFUL BY NATURE

Genesis 4:1–16; Genesis 6:5–6; Jeremiah 17:9–10; Romans 6:20–23

GENESIS 4:1–16
Cain Murders Abel

¹ The man was intimate with his wife Eve, and she conceived and gave birth to Cain. She said, "I have had a male child with the Lord's help." ² She also gave birth to his brother Abel. Now Abel became a shepherd of flocks, but Cain worked the ground. ³ In the course of time Cain presented some of the land's produce as an offering to the Lord. ⁴ And Abel also presented an offering—some of the firstborn of his flock and their fat portions. The Lord had regard for Abel and his offering, ⁵ but he did not have regard for Cain and his offering. Cain was furious, and he looked despondent.

⁶ Then the Lord said to Cain, "Why are you furious? And why do you look despondent? ⁷ If you do what is right, won't you be accepted? But if you do not do what is right, sin is crouching at the door. Its desire is for you, but you must rule over it."

⁸ Cain said to his brother Abel, "Let's go out to the field." And while they were in the field, Cain attacked his brother Abel and killed him.

⁹ Then the Lord said to Cain, "Where is your brother Abel?"

"I don't know," he replied. "Am I my brother's guardian?"

¹⁰ Then he said, "What have you done? Your brother's blood cries out to me from the ground! ¹¹ So now you are cursed, alienated from the ground that opened its mouth to receive your brother's blood you have shed. ¹² If you work the ground, it will never again give you its yield. You will be a restless wanderer on the earth."

¹³ But Cain answered the Lord, "My punishment is too great to bear! ¹⁴ Since you are banishing me today from the face of the earth, and I must hide from your presence and become a restless wanderer on the earth, whoever finds me will kill me."

¹⁵ Then the Lord replied to him, "In that case, whoever kills Cain will suffer vengeance seven times over." And he placed a mark on Cain so that whoever found him would not kill him. ¹⁶ Then Cain went out from the Lord's presence and lived in the land of Nod, east of Eden.

GENESIS 6:5–6
Judgment Decreed

⁵ When the Lord saw that human wickedness was widespread on the earth and that every inclination of the human mind was nothing but evil all the time, ⁶ the Lord regretted that he had made man on the earth, and he was deeply grieved.

JEREMIAH 17:9–10

⁹ "The heart is more deceitful than anything else,
and incurable—who can understand it?

¹⁰ I, the Lord, examine the mind,
I test the heart
to give to each according to his way,
according to what his actions deserve."

ROMANS 6:20–23

²⁰ For when you were slaves of sin, you were free with regard to righteousness. ²¹ So what fruit was produced then from the things you are now ashamed of? The outcome of those things is death. ²² But now, since you have been set free from sin and have become enslaved to God, you have your fruit, which results in sanctification—and the outcome is eternal life! ²³ For the wages of sin is death, but the gift of God is eternal life in Christ Jesus our Lord.

NOTES

The heart is more deceitful than anything else, and incurable—who can understand it? JEREMIAH 17:9

THE PERSON OF JESUS

In Matthew 16:15, Jesus asked His disciples, "Who do you say that I am?" When we look at how Jesus is presented in the Bible, we discover this is the most important question any of us can ask.

Jesus is the eternal Son of God.

Jesus, the Son of God, is a coequal member of the Trinity, along with the Father and the Holy Spirit. He has existed for all eternity. He refers to God as His Father, and the Father refers to Jesus as His Son.

PS 102:27; IS 9:6–7; MT 3:17; 16:15–16; 27:54; MK 1:1; LK 22:70–71; JN 5:18; 8:24; HEB 1:3; 13:8; RV 22:13

Jesus is God who became human.

Jesus is both fully God and fully man. The deity and humanity of Jesus are displayed through the testimony of the New Testament, which presents Him as the perfect mediator to intercede between sinful humanity and a holy God.

MT 2:11; MK 8:27–30; LK 9:28–36; JN 1:1–2, 14; 20:28; GL 4:4

Jesus is the Christ, the Messiah, Savior of sinners.

Jesus is the Messiah. He is the one appointed by God and empowered by the Holy Spirit to deliver humanity from our sin and rebellion against God.

IS 7:14; MT 1:22–23; 16:15–17; 26:63–64; MK 14:61–62; LK 9:20; JN 4:25–26; 20:31; 2TM 1:10

Jesus is the focus of Scripture and head of the Church.

All of Scripture focuses on Jesus and what He has done to reconcile humankind to God. He is the head of the visible Church, which He refers to as His bride.

LK 24:44; 1CO 6:19–20; EPH 1:22–23; 2:20; 5:23; COL 2:19; HEB 3:1–6; RV 19:7–9; 21:9

Jesus is the King who rules over heaven and earth.

Jesus has all authority in heaven and on earth. No person or thing is above Him. No power or authority can overcome Him. Jesus will reign over the new heavens and new earth forever.

MT 4:11; 28:20; JN 8:18; PHP 2:9–11; COL 1:18; HEB 1:2

DAY 5

WE CANNOT SAVE OURSELVES

*Isaiah 24:1–6; Matthew 19:16–22; Romans 8:5–11, 18–25;
Hebrews 7:26–28; Hebrews 9:22*

ISAIAH 24:1–6

The Earth Judged

¹ Look, the Lord is stripping the earth bare
and making it desolate.
He will twist its surface and scatter its inhabitants:
² people and priest alike,
servant and master,
female servant and mistress,
buyer and seller,
lender and borrower,
creditor and debtor.
³ The earth will be stripped completely bare
and will be totally plundered,
for the Lord has spoken this message.

⁴ The earth mourns and withers;
the world wastes away and withers;
the exalted people of the earth waste away.
⁵ The earth is polluted by its inhabitants,
for they have transgressed teachings,
overstepped decrees,
and broken the permanent covenant.
⁶ Therefore a curse has consumed the earth,
and its inhabitants have become guilty;
the earth's inhabitants have been burned,
and only a few survive.

Continued

MATTHEW 19:16–22

The Rich Young Ruler

16 Just then someone came up and asked him, "Teacher, what good must I do to have eternal life?"

17 "Why do you ask me about what is good?" he said to him. "There is only one who is good. If you want to enter into life, keep the commandments."

18 "Which ones?" he asked him.

Jesus answered: Do not murder; do not commit adultery; do not steal; do not bear false witness; 19 honor your father and your mother; and love your neighbor as yourself.

20 "I have kept all these," the young man told him. "What do I still lack?"

21 "If you want to be perfect," Jesus said to him, "go, sell your belongings and give to the poor, and you will have treasure in heaven. Then come, follow me."

22 When the young man heard that, he went away grieving, because he had many possessions.

ROMANS 8:5–11, 18–25

5 For those who live according to the flesh have their minds set on the things of the flesh, but those who live according to the Spirit have their minds set on the things of the Spirit. 6 Now the mind-set of the flesh is death, but the mind-set of the Spirit is life and peace. 7 The mind-set of the flesh is hostile to God because it does not submit to God's law. Indeed, it is unable to do so. 8 Those who are in the flesh cannot please God. 9 You, however, are not in the flesh, but in the Spirit, if indeed the Spirit of God lives in you. If anyone does not have the Spirit of Christ, he does not belong to him. 10 Now if Christ is in you, the body is dead because of sin, but the Spirit gives life because of righteousness. 11 And if the Spirit of him who raised Jesus from the dead lives in you, then he who raised Christ from the dead will also bring your mortal bodies to life through his Spirit who lives in you.

...

From Groans to Glory

18 For I consider that the sufferings of this present time are not worth comparing with the glory that is going to be revealed to us. 19 For the creation eagerly waits with anticipation for God's sons to be revealed. 20 For the creation was subjected to futility—not willingly, but because of him who subjected it—in the hope 21 that the creation itself will also be set free from the bondage to decay into the glorious freedom of God's children. 22 For we know that the whole creation has been groaning together with labor pains until now. 23 Not only that, but we ourselves who have the Spirit as the firstfruits—we also groan within ourselves, eagerly waiting for adoption, the redemption of our bodies. 24 Now in this hope we were saved, but hope that is seen is not hope, because who hopes for what he sees? 25 Now if we hope for what we do not see, we eagerly wait for it with patience.

HEBREWS 7:26–28

26 For this is the kind of high priest we need: holy, innocent, undefiled, separated from sinners, and exalted above the heavens. 27 He doesn't need to offer sacrifices every day, as high priests do—first for their own sins, then for those of the people. He did this once for all time when he offered himself. 28 For the law appoints as high priests men who are weak, but the promise of the oath, which came after the law, appoints a Son, who has been perfected forever.

HEBREWS 9:22

According to the law almost everything is purified with blood, and without the shedding of blood there is no forgiveness.

NOTES

We also groan within ourselves, eagerly waiting for adoption, the redemption of our bodies. ROMANS 8:23

DAY 6

GRACE DAY

In the beginning was the Word, and the Word was with God, and the Word was God. He was with God in the beginning. All things were created through him, and apart from him not one thing was created that has been created. In him was life, and that life was the light of men. That light shines in the darkness, and yet the darkness did not overcome it.

JOHN 1:1–5

Use today to pray, rest, and reflect on this week's reading, giving thanks for the grace that is ours in Christ.

DAY 7

WEEKLY TRUTH

Scripture is God-breathed and true. When we memorize it, we carry the gospel with us wherever we go.

This week we will memorize a verse that acknowledges sin's consequences and points us to the hope found in Jesus.

For the wages of sin is death, but the gift of God is eternal life in Christ Jesus our Lord.

ROMANS 6:23

Find the corresponding memory card in the back of this book.

REDEMPTION

For you are saved by grace through faith, and this is not from yourselves; it is God's gift—not from works, so that no one can boast.

EPHESIANS 2:8-9

DAY 8

JESUS LIVED, DIED, AND ROSE FROM THE GRAVE

John 3:16–17; Matthew 15:29–31; Luke 18:31–33; John 19:28–30; Romans 5:6–11; Philippians 2:5–11

JOHN 3:16–17

ⁱ⁶ "For God loved the world in this way: He gave his one and only Son, so that everyone who believes in him will not perish but have eternal life. ¹⁷ For God did not send his Son into the world to condemn the world, but to save the world through him."

MATTHEW 15:29–31
Healing Many People

²⁹ Moving on from there, Jesus passed along the Sea of Galilee. He went up on a mountain and sat there, ³⁰ and large crowds came to him, including the lame, the blind, the crippled, those unable to speak, and many others. They put them at his feet, and he healed them. ³¹ So the crowd was amazed when they saw those unable to speak talking, the crippled restored, the lame walking, and the blind seeing, and they gave glory to the God of Israel.

LUKE 18:31–33
The Third Prediction of His Death

³¹ Then he took the Twelve aside and told them, "See, we are going up to Jerusalem. Everything that is written through the prophets about the Son of Man will be accomplished. ³² For he will be handed over to the Gentiles, and he will be mocked, insulted, spit on; ³³ and after they flog him, they will kill him, and he will rise on the third day."

JOHN 19:28–30
The Finished Work of Jesus

²⁸ After this, when Jesus knew that everything was now finished that the Scripture might be fulfilled, he said, "I'm thirsty." ²⁹ A jar full of sour wine was sitting there; so they fixed a sponge full of sour wine on a hyssop branch and held it up to his mouth.

³⁰ When Jesus had received the sour wine, he said, "It is finished." Then bowing his head, he gave up his spirit.

ROMANS 5:6–11
Those Declared Righteous Are Reconciled

⁶ For while we were still helpless, at the right time, Christ died for the ungodly. ⁷ For rarely will someone die for a just person—though for a good person perhaps someone might even dare to die. ⁸ But God proves his own love for us in that while we were still sinners, Christ died for us. ⁹ How much more then, since we have now been declared righteous by his blood, will we be saved through him from wrath. ¹⁰ For if, while we were enemies, we were reconciled to God through the death of his Son, then how much more, having been reconciled, will we be saved by his life. ¹¹ And not only that, but we also rejoice in God through our Lord Jesus Christ, through whom we have now received this reconciliation.

PHILIPPIANS 2:5–11
Christ's Humility and Exaltation

⁵ Adopt the same attitude as that of Christ Jesus,

⁶ who, existing in the form of God,
did not consider equality with God
as something to be exploited.
⁷ Instead he emptied himself
by assuming the form of a servant,
taking on the likeness of humanity.
And when he had come as a man,
⁸ he humbled himself by becoming obedient
to the point of death—
even to death on a cross.
⁹ For this reason God highly exalted him
and gave him the name
that is above every name,
¹⁰ so that at the name of Jesus
every knee will bow—
in heaven and on earth
and under the earth—
¹¹ and every tongue will confess
that Jesus Christ is Lord,
to the glory of God the Father.

NOTES

DAY 9

JESUS CALLS US TO FAITH AND REPENTANCE

Psalm 51; Joel 2:12–13; Mark 1:14–15; Romans 5:1–2; Romans 10:9–10

PSALM 51

A Prayer for Restoration

For the choir director. A psalm of David, when the prophet Nathan came to him after he had gone to Bathsheba.

1 Be gracious to me, God,
according to your faithful love;
according to your abundant compassion,
blot out my rebellion.
2 Completely wash away my guilt
and cleanse me from my sin.
3 For I am conscious of my rebellion,
and my sin is always before me.
4 Against you—you alone—I have sinned
and done this evil in your sight.
So you are right when you pass sentence;
you are blameless when you judge.
5 Indeed, I was guilty when I was born;
I was sinful when my mother conceived me.

6 Surely you desire integrity in the inner self,
and you teach me wisdom deep within.
7 Purify me with hyssop, and I will be clean;
wash me, and I will be whiter than snow.
8 Let me hear joy and gladness;
let the bones you have crushed rejoice.
9 Turn your face away from my sins
and blot out all my guilt.

10 God, create a clean heart for me
and renew a steadfast spirit within me.
11 Do not banish me from your presence
or take your Holy Spirit from me.
12 Restore the joy of your salvation to me,
and sustain me by giving me a willing spirit.
13 Then I will teach the rebellious your ways,
and sinners will return to you.

14 Save me from the guilt of bloodshed, God—
God of my salvation—
and my tongue will sing of your righteousness.
15 Lord, open my lips,
and my mouth will declare your praise.
16 You do not want a sacrifice, or I would give it;
you are not pleased with a burnt offering.
17 The sacrifice pleasing to God is a broken spirit.
You will not despise a broken and humbled heart, God.

18 In your good pleasure, cause Zion to prosper;
build the walls of Jerusalem.
19 Then you will delight in righteous sacrifices,
whole burnt offerings;
then bulls will be offered on your altar.

JOEL 2:12–13

God's Call for Repentance

12 Even now—
    this is the LORD's declaration—
turn to me with all your heart,
with fasting, weeping, and mourning.
13 Tear your hearts,
not just your clothes,
and return to the LORD your God.
For he is gracious and compassionate,
slow to anger, abounding in faithful love,
and he relents from sending disaster.

MARK 1:14–15

Ministry in Galilee

14 After John was arrested, Jesus went to Galilee, proclaiming the good news of God: 15 "The time is fulfilled, and the kingdom of God has come near. Repent and believe the good news!"

ROMANS 5:1–2

Faith Triumphs

1 Therefore, since we have been declared righteous by faith, we have peace with God through our Lord Jesus Christ. 2 We have also obtained access through him by faith into this grace in which we stand, and we rejoice in the hope of the glory of God.

ROMANS 10:9–10

9 If you confess with your mouth, "Jesus is Lord," and believe in your heart that God raised him from the dead, you will be saved. 10 One believes with the heart, resulting in righteousness, and one confesses with the mouth, resulting in salvation.

NOTES

God, create a clean heart for me and renew a steadfast spirit within me.
PSALM 51:10

DAY 10

WE ARE SAVED BY GRACE THROUGH FAITH

Ephesians 2:1–10; Romans 3:21–26; Galatians 4:4–7; 1 Peter 1:3–9, 18–19; John 10:27–30

EPHESIANS 2:1–10
From Death to Life

¹ And you were dead in your trespasses and sins ² in which you previously lived according to the ways of this world, according to the ruler of the power of the air, the spirit now working in the disobedient. ³ We too all previously lived among them in our fleshly desires, carrying out the inclinations of our flesh and thoughts, and we were by nature children under wrath as the others were also. ⁴ But God, who is rich in mercy, because of his great love that he had for us, ⁵ made us alive with Christ even though we were dead in trespasses. You are saved by grace! ⁶ He also raised us up with him and seated us with him in the heavens in Christ Jesus, ⁷ so that in the coming ages he might display the immeasurable riches of his grace through his kindness to us in Christ Jesus. ⁸ For you are saved by grace through faith, and this is not from yourselves; it is God's gift— ⁹ not from works, so that no one can boast. ¹⁰ For we are his workmanship, created in Christ Jesus for good works, which God prepared ahead of time for us to do.

ROMANS 3:21–26
The Righteousness of God Through Faith

²¹ But now, apart from the law, the righteousness of God has been revealed, attested by the Law and the Prophets. ²² The righteousness of God is through faith in Jesus Christ to all who believe, since there is no distinction. ²³ For all have sinned and fall short of the glory of God. ²⁴ They are justified freely by his grace through the redemption that is in Christ Jesus. ²⁵ God presented him as an atoning sacrifice in his blood, received through faith, to demonstrate his righteousness, because in his restraint God passed over the sins previously committed. ²⁶ God presented him to demonstrate his righteousness at the present time, so that he would be righteous and declare righteous the one who has faith in Jesus.

GALATIANS 4:4–7

⁴ When the time came to completion, God sent his Son, born of a woman, born under the law, ⁵ to redeem those under the law, so that we might receive adoption as sons. ⁶ And because you are sons, God sent the Spirit of his Son into our hearts, crying, "*Abba*, Father!" ⁷ So you are no longer a slave but a son, and if a son, then God has made you an heir.

1 PETER 1:3–9, 18–19
A Living Hope

³ Blessed be the God and Father of our Lord Jesus Christ. Because of his great mercy he has given us new birth into a living hope through the resurrection of Jesus Christ from the dead ⁴ and into an inheritance that is imperishable, undefiled, and unfading, kept in heaven for you. ⁵ You are being guarded by God's power through faith for a salvation that is ready to be revealed in the last time. ⁶ You rejoice in this, even though now for a short time, if necessary, you suffer grief in various trials ⁷ so that the proven character of your faith—more valuable than gold which, though perishable, is refined by fire—may result in praise, glory, and honor at the revelation of Jesus Christ. ⁸ Though you have not seen him, you love him; though not seeing him now, you believe in him, and you rejoice with inexpressible and glorious joy, ⁹ because you are receiving the goal of your faith, the salvation of your souls.

...

¹⁸ For you know that you were redeemed from your empty way of life inherited from your fathers, not with perishable things like silver or gold, ¹⁹ but with the precious blood of Christ, like that of an unblemished and spotless lamb.

JOHN 10:27–30

²⁷ "My sheep hear my voice, I know them, and they follow me. ²⁸ I give them eternal life, and they will never perish. No one will snatch them out of my hand. ²⁹ My Father, who has given them to me, is greater than all. No one is able to snatch them out of the Father's hand. ³⁰ I and the Father are one."

NOTES

So you are no longer a slave but a son, and if a son, then God has made you an heir. GALATIANS 4:7

THE WORK OF JESUS

1

JESUS IS OUR PROPHET

2

JESUS IS OUR PRIEST

3

JESUS IS OUR KING

When both Scripture and early Church historians talk about the work of Jesus, they speak of Him as our Prophet, our Priest, and our King. These categories help us understand what Jesus has accomplished, and continues to accomplish, on our behalf.

1

JESUS IS OUR PROPHET

Prophets were sent to deliver messages from God. The message Jesus brought centers on how we can be reconciled to God. But Jesus did not just talk about salvation; He accomplished it. Jesus is both the Prophet and the message.

As our chief Prophet:

JESUS SPOKE, TAUGHT, AND ACTED WITH AUTHORITY

In His miracles and teaching, Jesus was recognized as one who spoke with authority about the nature and purpose of God.

MT 21:10-11; MK 1:22; LK 7:12-17; JN 6:14; 7:37-40

JESUS DELIVERED THE MESSAGE OF SALVATION

Jesus proclaimed to the entire world the way of salvation. He also is the way of salvation, and no one comes to God the Father unless they come through Him.

MT 7:24; 24:35; JN 1:1-5, 14; 8:31-32; 14:6; AC 4:12; 2TM 3:16-17

JESUS SHEPHERDS US IN THE TRUTH

Jesus protects, tends, and guides believers by the power and truth of His Word. He instructs us in the ways of God and leads us on the path to life.

PS 23; EZK 34:23; MT 18:12-14; JN 10:4-15; 1PT 2:25; RV 7:17

JESUS IS THE AUTHOR AND FINISHER OF OUR FAITH

Jesus made our salvation possible through His obedience to the Father. At the cross, He completed the work necessary for us to live in the freedom of the salvation He came to proclaim.

AC 3:15; EPH 1:13-14; PHP 1:6; HEB 2:10; 5:9; 12:2

2

JESUS IS OUR PRIEST

Priests stood as mediators between God and sinful humanity. They brought sacrifices before the Lord and led the people in repentance. As our priest, Jesus did not just offer a sacrifice to God on our behalf; He became the perfect and lasting offering for our sin. Jesus is both the Priest and the sacrifice.

As our High Priest:

JESUS BECAME OUR SACRIFICIAL LAMB

In living a perfect life and willingly giving Himself to suffering and death on the cross, Jesus was a perfect sacrifice for sin.

JN 1:29; RM 3:25–26; 1CO 5:7; EPH 5:2;
HEB 2:17; 9:14; 10:14; 1JN 2:2

JESUS PERFECTLY REPRESENTS US BEFORE GOD

Jesus perfectly represents humanity before God as our fully human, fully divine priest. He atoned for our sins through His own sinless life and sacrificial death. As our perfect representative, Jesus brings us into fellowship with God.

PS 110:1–4; RM 8:34; EPH 4:32; 1TM 2:5;
HEB 1:3; 4:14; 7:25–28; 8:1–2

JESUS REDEEMS BELIEVERS FROM THE DEBT OF SIN

Jesus redeems believers from death and bondage to sin through His death and resurrection, a ransom paid on our behalf.

HS 13:14; MK 10:45; RM 3:23–24; GL 4:4–5; EPH 1:7;
COL 2:14; 1PT 1:18–9; RV 5:9

JESUS RECONCILES BELIEVERS TO GOD

Through His death, Jesus brings peace to the severed relationship between people and God, and the world and God.

RM 5:10; 2CO 5:18–20; EPH 2:12–18; COL 1:19–22

JESUS IS OUR KING

Kings provided order, structure, security, and justice for their people. They commanded municipalities and armies to serve the needs of those under their care and protect them from enemies who would try to destroy them. Jesus does all of this for His people with perfect righteousness and absolute authority. Jesus is both the King and the servant of all.

As our reigning King:

JESUS SERVES HIS PEOPLE

Jesus temporarily set aside His full majesty in order to serve humanity and fulfill the will of God.

IS 42:1–4; MT 20:28; LK 22:27; JN 4:34; 13:11; PHP 2:6–7

JESUS SAVES HIS PEOPLE

Through the life, death, and resurrection of Jesus, believers are saved from the power of sin, the condemnation of the law, and the power of death.

JN 4:42; 6:40; AC 13:23; 15:11; RM 6:8–11; TI 1:4; PHP 3:20; 1PT 1:18–19

JESUS WILL JUDGE THE WORLD WITH PERFECT JUSTICE

In His life, death, and resurrection, Jesus executed judgment against evil. He will judge all humankind based on their response to Him.

JN 3:16–17; 5:22–27; AC 10:42; 2CO 5:10; 2TH 1:7–10; RV 20:11, 15

JESUS WILL REIGN FOREVER

Descended from the royal line of David, Jesus has been exalted by God to a place of power after His death, resurrection, and ascension. Jesus will rule over His kingdom forever.

2SM 7:13; IS 9:7; JR 23:5; DN 2:44; 7:14; LK 23:2–3; JN 18:36–37; 19:19–22; RV 1:5; 11:15

RESTORATION

"Look, I am making everything new."

REVELATION 21:5

DAY 11

JESUS SECURES OUR PEACE WITH GOD

John 14:27; Colossians 1:13–23; Colossians 3:1–4; 2 Corinthians 5:17–19; 1 Corinthians 15:51–57

JOHN 14:27
Jesus's Gift of Peace

"Peace I leave with you. My peace I give to you. I do not give to you as the world gives. Don't let your heart be troubled or fearful."

COLOSSIANS 1:13-23

¹³ He has rescued us from the domain of darkness and transferred us into the kingdom of the Son he loves. ¹⁴ In him we have redemption, the forgiveness of sins.

The Centrality of Christ

¹⁵ He is the image of the invisible God,
the firstborn over all creation.
¹⁶ For everything was created by him,
in heaven and on earth,
the visible and the invisible,
whether thrones or dominions
or rulers or authorities—
all things have been created through him and for him.
¹⁷ He is before all things,
and by him all things hold together.
¹⁸ He is also the head of the body, the church;
he is the beginning,
the firstborn from the dead,
so that he might come to have
first place in everything.
¹⁹ For God was pleased to have
all his fullness dwell in him,
²⁰ and through him to reconcile
everything to himself,
whether things on earth or things in heaven,
by making peace
through his blood, shed on the cross.

²¹ Once you were alienated and hostile in your minds expressed in your evil actions. ²² But now he has reconciled you by his physical body through his death, to present you holy, faultless, and blameless before him— ²³ if indeed you remain grounded and steadfast in the faith and are not shifted away from the hope of the gospel that you heard. This gospel has been proclaimed in all creation under heaven, and I, Paul, have become a servant of it.

COLOSSIANS 3:1-4
The Life of the New Man

¹ So if you have been raised with Christ, seek the things above, where Christ is, seated at the right hand of God. ² Set your minds on things above, not on earthly things. ³ For you died, and your life is hidden with Christ in God. ⁴ When Christ, who is your life, appears, then you also will appear with him in glory.

2 CORINTHIANS 5:17-19

¹⁷ Therefore, if anyone is in Christ, he is a new creation; the old has passed away, and see, the new has come! ¹⁸ Everything is from God, who has reconciled us to himself through Christ and has given us the ministry of reconciliation. ¹⁹ That is, in Christ, God was reconciling the world to himself, not counting their trespasses against them, and he has committed the message of reconciliation to us.

1 CORINTHIANS 15:51-57

⁵¹ Listen, I am telling you a mystery: We will not all fall asleep, but we will all be changed, ⁵² in a moment, in the twinkling of an eye, at the last trumpet. For the trumpet will sound, and the dead will be raised incorruptible, and we will be changed. ⁵³ For this corruptible body must be clothed with incorruptibility, and this mortal body must be clothed with immortality. ⁵⁴ When this corruptible body is clothed with incorruptibility, and this mortal body is clothed with immortality, then the saying that is written will take place:

Death has been swallowed up in victory.
⁵⁵ Where, death, is your victory?
Where, death, is your sting?

⁵⁶ The sting of death is sin, and the power of sin is the law. ⁵⁷ But thanks be to God, who gives us the victory through our Lord Jesus Christ!

NOTES

DAY 12

ALL CREATION WILL BE RESTORED

Psalm 24:1–2; Isaiah 65:17–25; Revelation 21:1–5, 22–27;
2 Peter 3:10–13

PSALM 24:1-2

¹ The earth and everything in it,
the world and its inhabitants,
belong to the Lord;
² for he laid its foundation on the seas
and established it on the rivers.

ISAIAH 65:17-25
A New Creation

¹⁷ "For I will create a new heaven and a new earth;
the past events will not be remembered or come to mind.
¹⁸ Then be glad and rejoice forever
in what I am creating;
for I will create Jerusalem to be a joy
and its people to be a delight.
¹⁹ I will rejoice in Jerusalem
and be glad in my people.
The sound of weeping and crying
will no longer be heard in her.
²⁰ In her, a nursing infant will no longer live
only a few days,
or an old man not live out his days.
Indeed, the one who dies at a hundred years old
will be mourned as a young man,
and the one who misses a hundred years
will be considered cursed.
²¹ People will build houses and live in them;
they will plant vineyards and eat their fruit.
²² They will not build and others live in them;
they will not plant and others eat.
For my people's lives will be
like the lifetime of a tree.
My chosen ones will fully enjoy
the work of their hands.
²³ They will not labor without success
or bear children destined for disaster,
for they will be a people blessed by the Lord
along with their descendants.
²⁴ Even before they call, I will answer;
while they are still speaking, I will hear.
²⁵ The wolf and the lamb will feed together,
and the lion will eat straw like cattle,
but the serpent's food will be dust!
They will not do what is evil or destroy
on my entire holy mountain,"
says the Lord.

REVELATION 21:1-5, 22-27
The New Creation

¹ Then I saw a new heaven and a new earth; for the first heaven and the first earth had passed away, and the sea was no more. ² I also saw the holy city, the new Jerusalem, coming down out of heaven from God, prepared like a bride adorned for her husband.

³ Then I heard a loud voice from the throne: Look, God's dwelling is with humanity, and he will live with them. They will be his peoples, and God himself will be with them and will be their God. ⁴ He will wipe away every tear from their eyes. Death will be no more; grief, crying, and pain will be no more, because the previous things have passed away.

⁵ Then the one seated on the throne said, "Look, I am making everything new." He also said, "Write, because these words are faithful and true."

...

²² I did not see a temple in it, because the Lord God the Almighty and the Lamb are its temple. ²³ The city does not need the sun or the moon to shine on it, because the glory of God illuminates it, and its lamp is the Lamb. ²⁴ The nations will walk by its light, and the kings of the earth will bring their glory into it. ²⁵ Its gates will never close by day because it will never be night there. ²⁶ They will bring the glory and honor of the nations into it. ²⁷ Nothing unclean will ever enter it, nor anyone who does what is detestable or false, but only those written in the Lamb's book of life.

2 PETER 3:10-13

¹⁰ But the day of the Lord will come like a thief; on that day the heavens will pass away with a loud noise, the elements will burn and be dissolved, and the earth and the works on it will be disclosed. ¹¹ Since all these things are to be dissolved in this way, it is clear what sort of people you should be in holy conduct and godliness ¹² as you wait for the day of God and hasten its coming. Because of that day, the heavens will be dissolved with fire and the elements will melt with heat. ¹³ But based on his promise, we wait for new heavens and a new earth, where righteousness dwells.

NOTES

―――

"For my people's lives will be like the lifetime of a tree. My chosen ones will fully enjoy the work of their hands." ISAIAH 65:22

DAY 13

GRACE DAY

For God was pleased to have all his fullness dwell in him, and through him to reconcile everything to himself, whether things on earth or things in heaven, by making peace through his blood, shed on the cross.

COLOSSIANS 1:19–20

Use today to pray, rest, and reflect on this week's reading, giving thanks for the grace that is ours in Christ.

DAY 14

WEEKLY TRUTH

Scripture is God-breathed and true. When we memorize it, we carry the gospel with us wherever we go.

This week we will memorize the key verse for this reading plan, a summary of the gospel of Jesus.

"For God loved the world in this way: He gave his one and only Son, so that everyone who believes in him will not perish but have eternal life. For God did not send his Son into the world to condemn the world, but to save the world through him."

JOHN 3:16–17

Find the corresponding memory card in the back of this book.

INVITATION

If you confess with your mouth, "Jesus is Lord," and believe in your heart that God raised him from the dead, you will be saved.

ROMANS 10:9

RESPONSE

Use this page to write a prayer of response to what you've read in this study.

DOWNLOAD THE APP

STOP BY
shereadstruth.com

SHOP
shopshereadstruth.com

SEND A NOTE
hello@shereadstruth.com

CONNECT
#SheReadsTruth

SHE READS TRUTH *is a worldwide community of women who read God's Word together every day.*

Founded in 2012, She Reads Truth invites women of all ages to engage with Scripture through daily reading plans, online conversation led by a vibrant community of contributors, and offline resources created at the intersection of beauty, goodness, and Truth.

FOR THE RECORD

WHERE DID I STUDY?

- ○ HOME
- ○ OFFICE
- ○ COFFEE SHOP
- ○ CHURCH
- ○ A FRIEND'S HOUSE
- ○ OTHER

WHAT WAS I LISTENING TO?

ARTIST:

SONG:

PLAYLIST:

WHEN DID I STUDY?

MORNING

AFTERNOON

NIGHT

What did I learn?

WHAT WAS HAPPENING IN MY LIFE?

WHAT WAS HAPPENING IN THE WORLD?

| MONTH | DAY | YEAR |

END DATE